How to Create a Marketing Plan For a Small Business

A Step by Step Guide to Marketing Planning

By Meir Liraz

I0462850

Published by BizMove
www.bizmove.com

ISBN: 9781090430397

Table of Contents

MEIR LIRAZ

1. Introduction

The marketing plan is a problem-solving document. Skilled problem solvers recognize that a big problem is usually the combination of several smaller problems. The best approach is to solve each of the smaller problems first, thereby dividing the big problem into manageable pieces. Your marketing plan should take the same approach. It should be a guide on which to base decisions and should ensure that everyone in your organization is working together to achieve the same goals. A good marketing plan can prevent your organization from reacting to problems in a piecemeal manner and even help in anticipating problems.

Before your marketing plan can be developed, research must give you the basic guidelines: for whom you are designing your product or service (market segmentation), and exactly what that product or service should mean to those in the marketplace (market positioning). Below are some guidelines to help you develop a marketing plan to support the strategy you have selected for your organization.

2. Market Segmentation

Your marketing plan should recognize the various segments of the market for your product or service and indicate how to adjust your product to reach those distinct markets. Instead of marketing a product in one way to everyone, you must recognize that some segments are not only different, but better than others for your product. This approach can be helpful in penetrating markets that would be too broad and undefined without segmentation. No matter what you are making or selling, take the total market and divide it up like a pie chart. The divisions can be based on various criteria such as those listed below.

Demographics

This is the study of the distribution, density and vital statistics of a population, and includes such characteristics as

Sex.

Age.

Education.

Geographic location.

Home ownership versus rental.

Marital status.

Size of family unit.

Total income of family unit.

Ethnic or religious background.

Job classification blue collar versus salaried or professional.

Psychographics

This is the study of how the human characteristics of consumers may have a bearing on their response to products, packaging, advertising and public relations efforts. Behavior may be measured as it involves an interplay among these broad sets of variables:

Predisposition - What is there about a person's past culture, heredity or upbringing that may influence his or her ability to consider purchasing one new product or service versus another?

Influences - What are the roles of social forces such as education, peer pressure or group acceptance in dictating a person's consumption patterns?

Product Attributes - What the product is or can be made to represent in the minds of consumers has a significant bearing on whether certain segments will accept the concept. These attributes may be suggested by the marketer or perceived by the customer. Some typical ways of describing a product include:

Price/value perception - Is the item worth the price being asked?

Taste - Does it have the right amount of sweetness or lightness?

Texture - Does it have the accepted consistency or feel?

Quality - What can be said about the quality of the ingredients or lack of artificial ingredients?

Benefits - How does the consumer feel after using the product?

Trust - Can the consumer rely on this particular brand? What about the reputation of the manufacturer in standing behind the product?

Life-Style

Statements consumers make about themselves

through conspicuous consumption can be put to good use by research people who read the signals correctly. By studying behavioral variables, such as a person's use of time, services and products, researchers can identify some common factors that can predict future behavior.

3. Market Positioning

You must realize that your product or service cannot be all things to all people. Very few items on the market today have universal appeal. Even when dealing in basic commodities like table salt or aspirin, marketing people have gone to all sorts of extremes to create brand awareness and product differentiation. If your product or service is properly positioned, prospective purchasers or users should immediately recognize its unique benefits or advantages and be better able to assess it in comparison to your competition's offering. Positioning is how you give your product or service brand identification.

Positioning involves analyzing each market segment as defined by your research activities and developing a distinct position for each segment. Ask yourself how you want to appear to that segment, or what you must do for that segment to ensure that it buys your product or service. This will dictate different media and advertising appeals for each segment. For example, you may sell the same product in a range of packages or sizes, or make cosmetic changes in the product, producing private labels or selecting separate distribution channels to reach the various segments. Beer, for example, is sold on tap and in seven-ounce bottles, twelve-ounce cans and bottles, six-packs, twelve-packs, cases, and quart bottles and kegs of several sizes. The beer is the same but each package size may appeal to a separate market segment and have to be sold with a totally different appeal and through different retail outlets.

Remember that your marketing position can, and should, change to meet the current conditions of the market for your product. The ability of your company to adjust will be enhanced greatly by an up-to-date knowledge of the marketplace gained through continual monitoring. By having good data about your customers, the segments they fit into and the buying motives of those segments, you can select the position that makes the most sense.

While there are many possible marketing positions, most would fit into one of the following categories:

Positioning on specific product features - A very common approach, especially for industrial products. If your product or service has some unique features that have obvious value this may be the way to go.

Positioning on benefits - Strongly related to positioning on product features. Generally, this is more effective because you can talk to your customers about what your product or service can do for them. The features may be nice, but unless customers can be made to understand why the product will benefit them, you may not get the sale.

Positioning for a specific use - Related to benefit positioning. Consider Campbell's positioning of soups for cooking. An interesting extension is mood positioning: "Have a Coke and a smile." This works best when you can teach your customers how to use your product or when you use a promotional medium that allows a demonstration.

Positioning for user category - A few examples: "You've Come a Long Way Baby," "The Pepsi Generation" and "Breakfast of Champions." Be sure you show your product being used by models with whom your customers can identify.

Positioning against another product or a competing business - A strategy that ranges from implicit to explicit comparison. Implicit comparisons can be quite pointed; for example, Avis never mentions Hertz, but the message is clear. Explicit comparisons can take two major forms. The first form makes a comparison with a direct competitor and is aimed at attracting customers from the compared brand, which is usually the category leader. The second type does not attempt to attract the customers of the compared product, but rather uses the comparison as a reference point. Consider, for example, the positioning of the Volkswagen Dasher, which picks up speed faster than a Mercedes and has a bigger trunk than a Rolls Royce. This usually works to the advantage of the smaller business if you can capitalize on the tradition of cheering for the underdog. You can gain stature by comparing yourself to a larger competitor just as long as your customers remain convinced that you are trying harder.

Product class disassociation - A less common type of positioning. It is particularly effective when used to introduce a new product that differs from traditional products. Lead-free gasoline and tubeless tires were new product classes positioned against older products. Space-age technology may help you here. People have become accustomed to change and new products and are more willing to experiment than was true ten years ago. Even so, some people are more adventuresome and trusting than others and more apt to try a revolutionary product. The trick is to find out who are the potential brand switchers or experimenters and find out what it would take to get them to try your product. The obvious disadvantage of dealing with those who try new products is that they may move on to another brand just as easily. Brand loyalty is great as long as it is to your brand.

Hybrid bases - Incorporates elements from several types of positioning. Given the variety of possible bases for positioning, small business owners should consider the possibility of a hybrid approach. This is particularly true in smaller towns where there aren't enough customers in any segment to justify the expense of separate marketing approaches.

4. MARKETING PLAN WORKSHEET

This is the marketing plan of _____

I. MARKET ANALYSIS

A. Target Market - Who are the customers?

1. We will be selling primarily to (check all that apply):

Percent of Business

a. Private sector _____

b. Wholesalers _____

c. Retailers _____

d. Government _____

e. Other _____

2. We will be targeting customers by:

a. Product line/services. We will target specific lines

_____

b. Geographic area? Which areas?

_____

c. Sales? We will target sales of

_____

d. Industry? Our target industry is

_____

e. Other? _____

3. How much will our selected market spend on our type of product or service this coming year?

_____

B. Competition

1. Who are our competitors?

Name _____

Address _____

Years in Business _____

Market Share _____

Price/Strategy _____

Product/Service _____

Features _____

Name _____

Address _____

Years in Business _____

Market Share _____

Price/Strategy _____

Product/Service _____

Features _____

2. How competitive is the market?

High _____

Medium _____

Low _____

3. List below your strengths and weaknesses compared to your competition (consider such areas as location, size of resources, reputation, services, personnel, etc.):

Strengths

1_____

2_____

3_____

4_____

Weaknesses

1_____

2_____

3_____

4_____

C. Environment

1. The following are some important economic factors that will affect our product or service (such as country growth, industry health, economic trends, taxes, rising energy prices, etc.):

_____

_____

_____

2. The following are some important legal factors that will affect our market:

_____

_____

_____

3. The following are some important government factors:

_____

_____

_____

4. The following are other environmental factors that will affect our market, but over which we have no control:

_____

_____

_____

II. PRODUCT OR SERVICE ANALYSIS

A. Description

1. Describe here what the product/service is and what it does:

_____

_____

_____

B. Comparison

1. What advantages does our product/service have over those of the competition (consider such things

as unique features, patents, expertise, special training, etc.)?

_____

_____

_____

2. What disadvantages does it have?

_____

_____

_____

C. Some Considerations

1. Where will you get your materials and supplies?

_____

2. List other considerations:

_____

_____

_____

III. MARKETING STRATEGIES - MARKET

MIX

A. Image

1. First, what kind of image do we want to have (such as cheap but good, or exclusiveness, or customer-oriented or highest quality, or convenience, or speed, or ...)?

_____

B. Features

1. List the features we will emphasize:

a. _____

b. _____

c. _____

C. Pricing

1. We will be using the following pricing strategy:

a. Markup on cost _____ What % Markup? _____

b. Suggested price _____

c. Competitive _____

d. Below competition _____

e. Premium price _____

f. Other _____

2. Are our prices in line with our image?

YES ___ NO ___

3. Do our prices cover costs and leave a margin of profit?

YES ___ NO ___

D. Customer Services

1. List the customer services we provide:

a. _____

b. _____

c. _____

2. These are our sales/credit terms:

a. _____

b. _____

c. _____

3. The competition offers the following services:

a. _____

b. _____

c. _____

E. Advertising/Promotion

1. These are the things we wish to say about the business:

_____

_____

_____

2. We will use the following advertising/promotion sources:

1. Television _____

2. Radio _____

3. Online: Google (AdWords) / Facebook

4. Direct mail _____

5. Personal contacts _____

6. Trade associations _____

7. Newspaper _____

8. Magazines _____

9. Yellow Pages _____

10. Billboard _____

11. Other _____

3. The following are the reasons why we consider the media we have chosen to be the most effective:

_____

_____

www.ingramcontent.com/pod-product-compliance
Lightning Source LLC
Chambersburg PA
CBHW072311170526
45158CB00003BA/1279